NEEDLES AND NEEDS

Poems

David Shevin

Midwest Writers Series
Bottom Dog Press
Huron, Ohio

ISBN 0-933087-30-6 $6.95 (soft)
ISBN 0-933087-32-2 $16.95 (cloth)

Acknowledgements

Gratitude to the editors who saw fit to first print many of these
poems.

Agenda Reports (Cincinnati): "On The Death of William B.
Shockley"; *Always a River*: "The Bridge I Used to Drive Across";
Chrysanthemum: "Poem Beginning With a Line By Emma
Lazarus"; *Confluence*: "Animal Heat," "Bright Life All Around";
Crazy River: "Forms of Witness"; *CutBank*: "Why East and West
Don't Understand One Another"; *Exquisite Corpse*: "Coyote and
the Flower Farm," "Planning for the Past"; *G.W. Review*: "Needles
and Needs"; *Headlands Journal*: "The New Brood, Midseason";
The Heartlands Today I: "En Afición, Está Despedida," "Kanawha
Grey Morning," "What Funny, Olive Drab"; *Light*: "Dead Horse
Breeder Raises a Ruckus With a Beneficiary"; *Mid-American
Review*: "Overdue Letter"; *The New Review*: "The Wives of the
Saints"; *Poetry USA*: "Driving Out of Seneca County"; *Rain City
Review*: "It Could Happen"; *Sisyphus*: "Count to Three, Count to
Twelve," "The Sendings Away," "William Walker XVIII"; *Visions:
International*: "Skink," *Xavier Review:* "The Music of Asian
Carolina."
"On the Death of William B. Shockley" was included in the
anthology *Eighty on the 80s* (Ashland Poetry Press, 1990).
"Planning for the Past" was reprinted in *The Heartlands Today* ,
and "The Sendings Away" in *Rage Before Pardon*.

Grateful thanks are also due to the Headlands Center for the
Arts, where beauty, time and nurture were provided to work on
this manuscript.
Deepest thanks are also due to the Ohio Arts Council, for the
Individual Artists Fellowship during 1991-2, when many of the
poems, and much of the editing for this volume were completed.
John Crawford was good enough to offer a close, careful and con-
structive critique of an early draft of this manuscript.
Cover: "Paolo and Francesca," pencil sketch by William Blake,
c.1826. From *Drawings of William Blake*, selected and edited by
Sir Geoffrey Keynes (Dover Publications, 1970). Reprinted by
permission of the publisher.

CONTENTS

I. Animal Heat

II. Needles

III. Needs

ANIMAL HEAT

for Nathan Shevin, 1918-91.

How far that little candle throws his beams!
So shines a good deed in a naughty world.

(***The Merchant of Venice***, V, i)

Five and Ten

"Would you change me two tens for a five?"
asked a comrade, a loyalist long with the Party.
"You see? And that's just what the socialist
countries have done." You never know how they'll
lie up or lie down, or what can be sold, you
prisoners of starvation. My dad could not sell
but tried like a racer. Nat the goodnatured guppy
in barracuda water. He rose and lay down
with the revolutions of his parents, conceived 1917
and gone in late 1991. While there was a Soviet Union
there was my father, the complex and tearful
and weakhearted bear. The sleepless volunteer
who worked for the schools when his own bank was empty
who angered the days he traded the market all day
and came home with his hand full of beans
and a promise. "They're trading their productive
capacities for a false bill of sale," my comrade says
in full confidence, experienced enough to recognize
the dash of hope against diamond walls, the memory
long as the night that he cried and he tossed at the fear
in his heart when his life was threatened for petitioning
against the execution of the Rosenbergs. Dust flew
in his mouth in a dream of his own violent end
and anonymous letters splashed hammer and sickle
with curses and lightning.

How I wanted to tell him what was possible in hope
and the personal gesture, that Nat saw warm mornings
before frost and silence. Retirement treated him well,
the man bilked by registers, account books
and a weakened heart muscle that claimed pride
at last. The remnants of last night's revolution
fill the air and the airwaves. October, the year
that my father's began, the provisional government

closed the newspaper *Rabochy Put*, the Red Guard
took the Warsaw Station. Grandmother planned to cook
in a restaurant. Look to that infant! Now walking
on weak legs. A sweet bear, who climbs up
to Jack London Park, is amazed by the old films
of thoroughbreds, recounting how moving it was
to watch the great author in sentiment over his animals.
"If the museum wasn't closing, you could watch him
discussing genetics with Burbank, and kissing his pigs."
The younger anger was all last season's cobwebs.
The failures and winnings were soup for night's chance.
"He held the piglet just like a child," said the bear
who held me that same way. Yes, comrade, bright moments
await us still in this short life where history
is as impersonal as a train station in Jersey
where a woman can pack a sandwich for her work
and worry where she's put it while lying
on tiles on the restroom floor giving birth
to a son, to a husband and father.

The bear said, "Drohichen, where my parents came from
was a place where they always liked it better
if the Polish Army was occupying instead of the Russian.
The winters, after all, are much colder in Russia."
I tell this to my comrade, the one who's alive
and obsesses with memory of hard battle, small gain.
It's a hard, hard humor that dying smiles back with
so funny we both forgot to laugh. What sense blinked
from stars that night when we rode with the coffin
and talked to the earth? Is it a logic that a man
is a guppy before he's a bear, that birth in a train
station restroom can grow into love so wrenching
that gone it's as cold as a stopped heart? In Russia
new entrepreneurs wrest morals from mayhem, at war
with morality that can't comprehend markup.
This world is a wish. This world is a moment of father

another of comrade, and many of wind. Another night
instead of fingering guitar strings or turning fresh pages
I'll find a public place in a station or forest
where the voices will wish a strong walk to a gentle bear
whose legs and whose heart aren't quit yet. Not yet.
This is one world, and this is one wish.

Animal Heat

October. 1886.
Shayna Fruma argued that her daughter Ida
should learn to read in this new and wonderful America.
"It's a new world and a girl should be schooled."
"What school?" countered Abram.
"She'll just be a teacher.
She'll be too smart for us."

Ida traded thimbles and thread
on the streetcorner, and by ten years old
she did finishing work at home for shirts
from the plant.
After some years she worked in the plant itself

and her brother-in-law there took *Der Tag*
and everyone argued suffrage, argued wages
and anarchism. Ida learned about reading, too.

The Forward endorsed Eugene Debs from his prison cell.
Isaac Merrit Singer's machines wedded fabrics
and buttons of bone.

Cold rains kept polishing Herman Street
and Lake Avenue. Saturdays the shop closed.
When havdalah separated the sacred from the profane
the girls frequently found a catch in the voice
going one more time
to work on Sunday.

April. 1913.
The Women's Trade Union League sent Leonora O'Reilly
to Rochester from Brooklyn. Scrabbling
for empowerment in empire, O'Reilly was —

rubbing againt the class grain and preaching
the suffrage cause in the trades meetings.
10,000 were about to march for the woman vote
in New York and then Ida wrote her congratulation:

> *nothing could pleas me more then to be with you*
> *and participate in this noble event, but as I could not be there*
> *my spirit was there just the same ... The girls Local*
> *of the garment workers union gave a package party and dance*
> *for the striking garment workers in Canada. We cleared*
> *one hundred and twenty five dollars which we think is very good...*

and O'Reilly dispatched thanks with copies of the League's
publication, *Labor and Leisure*. Look! Look what had been
in the paper! After Triangle, there were strikes
in New York. The cloakmakers signed with I.L.G.W.U.
In Chicago, the workers at Hart, Schaffner & Marx
were leading the citywide strike.
How warm the idea: a workday of just eight hours!
Back home without the machines you know
a tailor worked as he had work.
Just for the clothes that were needed.

And the pages all found their good eyes
and their mouths. Animal heat
was the grease of machines.
The mills of God were grinding fast.
Words found their way back
as ink became air became action: could Ida
represent the magazine in Rochester,
Lenore wanted to know.

Tables and chairs and some needles, a shawl.
Work had piled up and the air had no song
but it strained at the phrasing as Ida declined,

As I am not a lady of leisure.and every minute of my time
is taken.so I could not take their propersition but...
I am going to prescribe for one myself...I quite agree
with the auther, for it is true we need both things in order to
meet all that is required in life but the great fault
with our present system is that some have all the leisure
and the others has to labor to make up for the work
which they should do

and she paused. She considered her friends
and her work.

but I hope the time will soon come, when we all have leisure
as well as labor.

Starlings took flight as she licked the stamp.
The strike was still winning in Canada.
Abram and Shayna were both getting older
and Ida had not yet begun to keep company
with Sam who drove the coal delivery cart.
Oh Ida, my blood and my teacher,
your father was right when he asked "What school."

You can't drown water.
You can't burn fire.

Bright Life All Around

(Sam Drexler, 1886-1975)

Bright life all around, but in the house we had turtles
and goldfish. This country of jumps, yips and quirks
where animals walked their fur into houses
was something too breathy for Sam's view of progress.
Rochester preened much too pretty for industry.
One day Grandpa Sam uprooted the lilac bush,
tarred the spot over and sealed the black ground.
The next year the roses were cut from the trellis.
Marigold shine on blue time and rust pictures.

It almost didn't matter what industry made possible,
Sam would love it. His electric pencil sharpener
felled forests. His pushbutton opener for the garage door
sent boards up and down, down and up several times
before the car entered or exited. (Today a high school senior,
the son of a colleague, told me this story: "You wouldn't
believe the boneheads in Driver Ed. We had one flake
and she thought she'd get a ahead of the driver in front
on the highway. So she shifts into 'P' for 'Pass.'")

I thought of the wonder Sam held for mechanics.
"They can do that now?" he would ask. Yes he would,
because Sam understood subtle concepts,
like sweet-and-sour cooking. One day I asked Sam
what he had on the stove, and he looked through me
with the eye of a Rembrandt, that fixity, ease.
"This is pinapple-beet soup. Would you like
to try some?" The years of freeelance carpentry work
and hauling the coal in the horsedrawn cart

were past when I knew Sam. Memory shuffles through
autumns of coloring images, one on chiascuro another:
paisley tie in 1920 posed portrait, stiff suit

and rubber stamp on the rent check, years in a bathrobe
worn over grey trousers, and always so serious in an awe
ever deepening as the world retranslated into notes
of deafness. Yo, Sam! Look outside. There, there
in the Ohio alley. The guy with the dog. Never mind,
about the dog, I won't ask him in the house.

I know you don't like them. But check out what they're doing.
The guy has the dog on a leash for a walk. But he's the one,
not the dog, who's pissing on the garage.
Maybe they forgot who they are. What do you think?

I close my eyes, expecting an answer. I'm watching you
straighten your tie.

NEEDLES

A Samurai and a No-Swordsman were riding on a raft with some people when the Samurai challenged the No-Swordsman to a duel. The No-Swordsman replied, "Let's jump out when we get to the next island rather than fight on the raft and possibly hurt the others." When the raft drifted by an island, the Samurai jumped out. The No-Swordsman didn't and the raft moved on. I wonder who won the duel?

—Abbie Hoffman
"Free is the Revolution"

First Dance With the Jaguar

*Lo único eterno el cielo y el viento
y córazon de ayer*
—Tish Hinojosa, "Samba San Pedro"

I've never kissed a bear and I've never kissed a goon
But I can shake a chicken in the middle of the room.
Let's have a party! / I can remember the band
was singing crazy, like it was not the war or anything.
I was thirteen, and our teacher showed us a book
about what a woman was. It was wonderful book.
Dionisia sneaked it out of the school one Sunday
and I never studied harder with her. How could I talk
with my mother about such things: love at first sight,
menstruation, the spirit and sweat that meant more
than the cotton crop or the river? People had told me
that sex was something powdery. So until I met my husband
I was a naive. I was going to spread sex on myself
like a talc, like dry leaves over hard wood, as sure
as the docks on the *costa atlantica.* The triumph
and my marriage came both in the same year,
but what I remember today more than anything
was the dance that Tacho the potato farmer
staggered, jumped wild with me three years before.
The air where he moved smiled cane rum.
Children slapped their forearms around his forehead
as he'd shoulder them for a *cumbia,* moving native
to the norte music that the business owners sons
had learned how to play. "Let's have a party!"
they were singing over in English. I saw my figure
or soul in his sweat, or maybe my son who was to come.
I had no rum and just a taste of beer — I was still a child.
But I was drunk as a city parson on the night air.

15

Tacho was almost eighteen. His friends called him
"The Jaguar," because he'd trained so well at *soldado*.

Then I rediscovered the color of night, a mottle
with shadings of ghosts and the paintings of saints.
In three years we married. We went to the mountain waterfall.
I was still shy. I did not want the Jaguar to see me
without my clothes, even when we were alone.
He said that I would learn to open like a flower
when it is pollinated. I knew that terrible things
could happen in the world. I remembered that a soldier
had raped a girl, cut off her breasts, and drank her blood.
And maybe this is why I am clear today, then it was not so.
I was wishing for the truth in the book Dionisia snitched.
Youth is short lived, and education can make you believe
in the impossible. And sometimes now, in the mornings
when I am alone with the birds, I think of the night
of dances and powder. Then I was still anonymous,
and a book could still promise me dreams.

Planning for the Past

It's no secret the M & R's supposed to be a rough bar
and I'm a peaceful man. I've been coming here for years
and never had a part in any of the violent stuff. Tell you
why I sat here. You're my generation — no offense, I'm forty
and you seem like someone who would know my history,
not like most of them kids (and he shrugs toward the dart throwers)
who don't care about space travel or anything; what do you think
of that telescope, anyway? I love to fly, wanted to fly in Nam
but they wouldn't have me. Three times they called me up,
and three times they turned me away. The physical would come
down at the forthouse in Columbus. The doc would say, "Squat down,"
we'd be a row of us naked, and one of my knees would rise,
rise higher than the other like a derrick pulling oil.
The doc would say "Go home" and they'd call me again. I'd want
to go because I believe in democracy, because people get
what they vote for here. Now I don't vote, but I believe
in this country. The guy who won has advisors up the ass —
he has thousands of advisors, so if he doesn't know what's
going on, who does? I don't like fighting, but if he says
the moon is a prune or the vaseline is gasoline, I believe it
because we elected him and he knows. You know what I like?

I like finches. I been keepin em four months now. You like
birds? I got six of em, three pair. They're tiny and fly
free in the apartment. I love to fly. They call me
the Birdman of Cary, that's where I do my finishing work.
Thought the pet shop at Six's ripped me when they sold
me the Cordon Bleus, because I was reading about a mark
the female's supposed to have at the neck. They told
me they had papers, this was a male and female pair and now
I've got these little blue eggs they nest on. If the chicks
don't have a mark and they're girls I might have a new strain
and I'm gonna sell em. They're beautiful. The Bleus don't call
except to trade places nesting. The others, Zebras from Australia,

quack all the time like ducks, like this: 'Quack! Quack!'
And the third pair, they're Society finches. They sing way back
in their throats like the opera. I hurt my knee once at football
and if the pain comes I listen to finches and I'm somewhere
else. The Societies got eggs, too. Pretty soon I'm gonna
be an uncle. I put these three cages together, but they're
always open. Did you know that finches will show affection?
And birds aren't supposed to domesticate. They're so tiny.
They sit on my shoulders like epaulets. They talk in my ears.

Skink

You've laid over from the travel
aching Pennsylvania grit
scraped from the ore's intestines.
Moon rising mostly full
in Molly Maguire's country.
For centuries, it seems the seamstress
Wheeling-Pittsburgh has been hemming
soot to the road's edge, snow rolling crazy
over muck road.

Willie lines a skinky combination
off two cushions, sinks the straggler,
brushes the eight toward the corner.
He works slowly, low on the table,
puts it in the pocket
his next time up. Willie's legally blind.
"If you needed a licence to drive a cue ball
then I'd be sunk," he says. He reorders
the lens in his good eye, focuses for a long time
to make sure he sees you. "Good game,"
he lies. You have four left on the table
and point that out. Willie shrugs.
"You can't always get what you want
unless you always want what you get."

That's what he does is order things,
and does that by words.
"You check the dictionary,"
he tells you. "Between the marvels
and the Maryknollers
is where you'll find the Marxists.
You look lower than a reprobate or a reptile,
you're sure to find a Republican."
"You're sly," you tell him
in the clouds and beerhall damp.

Beneath a cold buffalo of a mountain
with an iron scar in its wood
he asks of your life into later and later.
He's interested in tavellers.
Before leaving, he hands you the soapstone
and knife in his pocket, says you should
add a detail to the half-finished Jesus.
What's the momentum that carries him
from some thirties struggle when he was born
into the rocks he'll ride tomorrow at work
blinking his good eye at coal angels?
You can't tell, but you're the visitor
and this is the country where you take leave
while boys pitch a baseball back and forth in the snow.
Damn, you think.

Most anything can leap from the heart.

It Could Happen

Maybe in Omaha, the *World Journal* would report on the ashfall
of 9,998,009 B.C., approximately. Crowned cranes
and hornless rhinos and bone crushing dogs inhaled
the ash, it would say. It choked their lungs and buried their food
and poisoned their water. Nebraska then had been
lush and tropical. Four tusked elephants
and giraffe-camels and three-horned deer
and browsing horses planned their biological empires.
It could be that Nebraska was the Zimbabwe of the Mesozoic.

Maybe in California, late in the spring, redtailed hawks
would still restructure their nests. The fat redtop quail
would cower and flop, and in broad flight
the black carnivorous bird would catch an updraft, pose
with a long piece of string in its beak and bank across
the deep green of the hillside. Sunlight would winnow
the morning fog and the hawk's home would come into view
where sky lives. The address is always the spot on the spectrum
where greys turn to skyblues. This, too, could happen.

And maybe in Seneca County, Ohio, the virus that took
Mark's resistance would go scurry, too, somewhere blank and desolate.
The ravages in his teeth and eyes would get taken back. He'd play
playful music, laugh over again. His questioning stound
would replace all the fear of these last months. We could talk
about subjects other than how ill he'd become,
appreciate mixed cultures of national concerns in rural midwestness
that closes inside, like doors onto brick. Like jail cells
in crystallite. Histories in amber.

Maybe relinquishing chaos could be the new drama before us.
Maybe you and I too will be blessed with the
slowness in which we can fatten and harden, cultivate our old
        growth rings
as squat and as tall as the hardwoods this continent grew
in abundance. Look at me. It could happen. Anything.

Call Me Irresponsible

If you are not responsible
For anything, it is a kind of comfort

And a sadness that will never leave you.
—Patricia Goedicke, "Mountainside Farm"

"Cheer up!"
"Who?"
"Honk!"

"Cheer up!" "Who?" "Honk!" "Cheer up!" "Who?" "Honk!"
All night they were calling. The crickets. The horned owl.
The foghorn. Fog seethed and boiled over the bluffs
of Marin coast, so murky the deer and the bobcats
bumped into each other and asked to be excused. *"Cheer up!"*
"Who?" "Honk!" said the night.

It was into this night that you brought your wounds
all packed up in bundles and tied with frayed
ribbons. Your lover's false condolances (*cheer up*)
and your mother's timid, limiting advice (*honk*)
and your father's stern and wrongheaded lectures
(*Who?*) and the anger that said:

"You want me to do what?" and you threw the bundles
high, letting them scatter on sands at low tide.
It was a symbolic act for you, a statement
that for these items, you are no longer responsible.
There is a cool, irregular wind at your back
that's almost fingers and almost feathers.

Will the dawn break in ease and in comfort? the wind asks.
"Oh, yes!" you are sobbing. On dark waves
by Cuzcatlan by Salvador, the dead are smiling (*cheer up*).
Will the parcels wash out into brine, into green sea? "Yes! Yes!"

Waves wash oil over shore birds, and flight gets too heavy *(honk)*.
Will unweighted days fill with pleasure, and time go

unchecked by guilty history? "Yes!" Across the divide
there's a fire in the hole. But tomorrow will dawn
— this you know as you head for the small, blue Accord
and tomorrow a loving world beckons in which television
can tell you the right stuff to buy
and your singular job will be flipping the dials.

Why East and West Don't Understand One Another

In one of his poems, Czeslaw Milosz writes of a *maral*
— a small Siberian deer — who bellows in the crisp
air beneath an October moon. There you have it.
That's why East and West don't understand one another.

In America our deer don't bellow. They snort
and they grunt at mating season. They scare the fizz
out of you if you surprise one while walking through the woods.
They run perfectly, as luminous as...as...as running deer.

American deer can't even imagine their small, bellowing cousins.
What would they bellow? ask bucks in Muskingum County.
"Bambi, get out of that ivy. You'll get your fall coat all stained!"
or "Put out that cigarette. Only you can prevent forest fires."

It doesn't compute. So the guys talk instead of important
deer history. How the great deep hypnotist Antlarian
would always use headlights in his act. What does a Siberian
bellowing deer look like? Has he a froglike sac

engineered for bellowing, generations of genes selected
for power projection: deer howls across the tundra?
What does he bellow? Does he cry angst and loss
like the great Russian poets?

  "Wooden Russia, my childhood ran merry
  As a fawn near the Don through my sweetwater spring.
  Now I age; the fat peasant hunter has me wary.
  How we suffered the season when Ivan was king!"

So much melodrama! No wonder the practical does in Ohio
don't dwell on that rot. They're too busy picking up
after the guys' fallen antlers, or drawing up forage lists
or clearing the appointments with the hoof and cud specialists.

And some Soviet intellectuals idealize our country,
a land where the deer keep their mouths shut. How pure!
And when I ask my friends just what have they been thinking
about the Siberian bellowing deer, they have little to say.

They've blocked it from their minds. This is what's called "denial."
That's why East and West don't understand one another.

Forms of Witness

*And the ass saw the Angel of the Lord standing
in the way, with his sword drawn in his hand;
and the ass turned aside out of the way, and
went into the field; and Bil' am smote the ass,
to make her turn into the way.*
—**Numbers** XXII:23

There are as many forms of witness
as species of belief — an annual distance contest
in one Andes village is called
The Crawling on the Belly for the Virgin.
This may last for three days.
On Lakewood Beach on the Erie shore
the three day summerfest begins with eighty marines
("Screaming Marines," as reported in the *Lorain Journal*)
storming the shore, born from four cruisers off the USS Boulder
firing rounds from automatic weapons, sending up smokescreens,
and crawling on their bellies.

The public witness loves the event. Twenty thousand
gather and cheer and bow heads
when the Navy Band Atlantis plays the National Anthem.
This song began as a witness to alcoholic excess,
"To Anachraeon in Heaven." In misted August sunrise
beside the coal plant on the lake, a sober driven multitude
choruses of bombs bursting in air as a gull
fat as a king brushes electric on the water.
Willie Hailey, son of J.K., asks his dad to protect
a small handful of spent cartridges. "See son?
I told you they were using real bullets."

Willie blows a siren with his lip on a hollow casing tip.
A dog lifts from the lake edge and gallumphs back in near-waltz.
If asked, there are many who downgrade the dissidents
aching for funds to build people, not rifles

trading recipes for breads minus gunpowder —
"They are to be ignored and pitied," says Allen Ashbolt.
J.K.'s more forceful: "Our nation was founded
on God's infallible word. They must be turned into the way,
even if it means by force." If not asked, the echoes fly low
amid the moorings. I too was detained by these guns,
that time in the hands of a Salvadoran kid in Guazapa

and he looked to be fifteen years old. He looked less
the *militar santo* than shrunken — was he doubting too
the infallible word? War there was not a carnival;
but is reminder necessary? Bil'am's ass knew that one.
At the gazebo, beside the "Unifying Ohio for Peace" sign,
decency's veterans anger in the weltering cheers.
Above the deep tan of Erie carbon and sand
Mayor Alex Olejko arrives in his wheelchair.
"I hope Cleveland will realize this is happening,"
he proclaims. Another proclamation skims the Pacific
from Cristiani's prison in San Miguel.

It is the scream of many voices.
There are no discernable words.

Dead Horse Breeder Raises a Ruckus With a Beneficiary

—front page headline, *Wall Street Journal*

The guy who used to room with my brother
and who never came up with his half of the rent
invites me to visit him, looks sycophantic
and beaten at once, as though the kid you could feed
for just dollars a month in the magazine ad
had grown suddenly old. I think of the husbandry
entrepreneur who was raising dead horses.
The bright newborn carcass is perfect for flogging.
The eyes don't react to cold glances or boredom
or violence or madness. To think he would never
have started the business if not for poor hearing!
His father advised him on options in music
for a son who's tone deaf. The kid was serious.
He started his enterprise. "No, no," said Dad,
"I said 'beating,' not 'breeding'!" Still sales
were contracted through businesses, government,
colleges — the new dead horse industry sparked
and took fire, grew to legend.
Now I face my once colleague, gone wretched
with past dues. He beats on his dead horse.
His eyes aren't even showing he knows what he does
but reflect a sad movie, so daftly familiar:
the leather strap rising and falling on dust.

On the Death of William B. Shockley

When Billy B.S. was approached by his critics
his manners were brusque and not soft Dr. Spockly.
They wanted to know why his burgeoning offspring
were no mental giants, thinking quick-as-a-rockly:
In fact, one son tested an I.Q. which fell
between Kellogg's Pop Tarts and a bundle of broccoli.
Ambition for that one was that he'd mature
as a goal post, or play Puck in Detroit ice hockley.
But quick with an answer, the "dysgenics" theorist
stood tall in his tight genes and spoke out: "Unlockely,
my dumb first wife's traits are intelligence coded
at levels Doc Watson's, while mine are Sherlockly."
Bill's preaching on race differentials in thinking
weren't spoiled 'cuz his kids were not chip-off-the-blockly.
They were matched by a nerve guaranteeing long years
of right wing celebrity. But his prostate got pockly
with cancer. He died. Still, his sperm legacy
is preserved in small lab vials in old Little Rockly.
The system he forwarded? Sterilization
of low intellects and the outlaws, the jockly,
the ill. If our luck will improve in this world
power failures will dwindle our stockly of Shockley.

29

"Nixon library to limit data, restrict access

> *...the library will also lack a full set of memos, letters,*
> *and other documents from Nixon's White House years when it*
> *opens later this month."*
>
> —**Associated Press**, 7/9/90

Y'know, I came to this library cuz I thought I could
find out something more about animals cuz my dad always said
this guy Nixon was a weasel and it takes one to know one, see.
Oh yeah? I know you are but what am I. Shut up. I'm trying
to ask the librarian a question. What have you got about this bird
they called Eagle Crow. What was he anyway? No. What kind
    of bird?
No, I'm not kidding
around.
Omigoood, what are you talking about, one of Woodward's
little jackanapes.
Or didn't you mean
jack-knives? I don't know what you're talking about. No, it' cuz
in natural sciences we have Mr. Hyrax (Right. Lucky me.)
Y'know
the one with the padded feet and he's always asking us to find out
weird things about animals. I think he's a zookeeper at home
or something. Like get this. Tomorrow's homework questions.

    Although the Tiger is not indigenous to Italy, the one
    we all know is named Tony. Why is this?

    How are the performing Rabbit Brothers, Eddie and Roger,
    related to Edward R. Burrow?

    Before Captain Kangaroo's promotion, had any of his species
    ever risen above Second Lieutenant?

And then there's this bonus question about the Eagle Crow. No,
how would I know that. It's Hydrox Cookies makes this stuff up,
    I swear.

I thought I told you to shut up.

Yeah, and he wants us to tell him where we get the information,
too. So you're just gunna shove us out of here? Yeah?

Maybe we can go to the Reagan Library in Seamy Valley and look up
that stuff we missed on inbreeding and newts. *Jeez.*

Some place this is.

I thought I was going to learn something about weasels.

The Wounded Birds

The wounded birds have been getting smaller.

For a moment their might filled the airwaves and air
the days when the skies rained Republicans. A Pennsylvania
patrician bird squawked big, then tumbled across a schoolyard.
A squat opportunistic parasite bird headed south,
and then slammed into flames with an astronaut bird.

How awful their flying, what bloodbellied markings, what terror
they made their trajectory! was all on my mind when a grackle
lit fast from the soyfield's edge on route 53. He caught fast
in a bluster of midspring midwest downdraft, and thought
of his balancing wing the moment he whapped
the right top of my windshield, skidded the hood
and was gone miles behind.

What blackness his color, and fastness his flight
in the wind's fleshy muscle, the machine's unforgiveness.
Imagine a red spot on mottle, a bruise on the window
that sighs as fields and factories fly past.

The car was new washed when I came home this morning.
On the porchstep, a fledgeling thrown somehow from its nest
— so tiny, it was hard to tell what sort of bird, a pigeon
with yellowgold bill — flopped and trembled in the new day's
sweltering sun. I reached and then drew back my hand,
having read that a mother bird may reject its touched
scented young. I took it to shade on some cardboard

gave it sugar water, poured into its heavenward, ravening
mouth through tiniest spoonfuls. It spoke and it trembled.
So light the grey down and so tiny the pinions,
so nervous the body that found its way over to nestle

on a makeshift nest of last year's leaves and this year's seeds
between the step's concrete and brick.

Come cool of the evening the bird looked some stronger.
The mouth gaped up huge for the blessing of water.
Will family come calling, or cats, or a fierce wind?
This is a prayer for wings stronger than senators.
This is a hope for a breath in life's future.
See the new feathers ruffling on red flush of skin.

What Funny, Olive Drab

Sun still rising on the olive groves,
North Central California. Grandfather Sun
is the only true shaman,
for he can walk through the snow
without leaving a mark. Three quarter moon
still high, toenail in flight.
Shadow of a farming truck wavers
and blinks on unblinking concrete.
These are funny places,
these west and north strains
of Mexico that try to pass English Only laws.
    Here the foolish radio
    runs its survey — what our soldiers
    want is bibles, "They can't
    get enough of them."
What funny. Our soldiers are hungry.
Soldiers always are.
And they never want for bibles.
    This far stretch past the Mission Trail
    Spanish names grow fewer.
Crag and rockface over treelines

    Why do shadows waver
    when the system holds so firm?

Poem Beginning With a Line By Emma Lazarus

Cheryl Lemmels was student editor of the literary
magazine at San Diego State University, 1978-9.
Since then, over 2,700 of her poems have been
published in **Kansas Quarterly, Webster Review,**
Hiram Poetry Review, Modern Maturity,
and many other journals.
—Contributor's note, *Crazyquilt*

Not like the brazen giant of Greek fame,
A new Colossus rose, though not by might
To rule, but numbers. How swiftly, like light-
Ning the zip codes and mail service! Shake
Poems from mailmen, teachers, electricians!
Pythagorus swoons when the countdown holds sway
On production, and still more poems sway
From the wellspring that knows no omissions
Or wastebaskets. "Fly! Fly to transcript and ink
My strong paper cranes, Calliope's cantos!
Let these lines of heroes protect as portmanteaus
The myth of our age, both the sweet and the stink!"
For nine years her muse always smiles, never sours
And a new poem finds print every twenty six hours.

The Bridge I Used to Drive Across

It was Cincinnati to Covington,
across the C's. The bridge I used
to drive across sang a low, unintelligible song.
It was as though the music wanted to come
apart beneath me, like a distant betrayal.

A shin banged on the bedframe or an open
drawer, intercepting an elbow. On one
February morning, barges passed with the ice,
started from McKeesport, and sailing the Ohio
to the Mississippi. From there out the Gulf,

across Panama, up the Pacific Coast,
to rest at the Hanford Nuclear Reservation.
The barges carried a nuclear reactor, gone old
and gone cold. It was one of the first experimental
lightwater models built by General Electric

and his faithful troops. From my union office
we saw the nuke clunking the bank passage
on its weird, stoney tumble downstream.
North of town at Fernald, the aquafir picked up
uranium tailings from the processing plant.

Years later, these backed up in toilets. Hanford
was a living sieve, and distant betrayals were bad cells
of the future. My bridge sang and bumped
in the midwinter winds and the river's dark shapes
rhumbaed future and far. Six people

were celebrating that night at the Jolly Inn.
There was dancing, and — why not? —
I guessed at the steps. A head full of unknown
and random direction, barge of hot rock tossing
crazy downriver. Look how I'm dancing!

It was probably dancing. And most of the way
 it led home.

Supreme Court Upholds Death Penalty

I dreamed I saw Joe Hill last night
dead as a doornail

Whom the Gods Would Destroy

Politics had always been the systematic organization of hatreds.
                                        —Henry Adams

The makers of bigbig play wild with small lives.
In Northern Kentucky, a sign writ in the English of puppies and
    insects:

Big Bone Lick State Park. Because this was a tar pit. You following?
No? Oh, I'll go back a step. See it was a tar pit and now

it's a park. See, they made it a park because here were big bones.
I mean bigbones, the hipbones of fossilized mastodons, critters

who left their big slow hips behind when they caught in the tar.
Why go lolling in tar? you ask? Just 'cause? Well, their operation

Just Cause was to get to the salt lick deep in and below
the organic ooze which just ain't there no more. Now you argue

it didn't take much to go fooling a mastodon. Hand him a salt fix,
he'll chase into anything, jungle or desert or bubblebath tar.

Trouble after finding the salt was he couldn't get out,
turned into Marathon's useful petrochemicals, fired us some engines

so we can go distances, check out his hips. "Read my hips,"
says dinosaur to visitor, who wonders at the cruelty that places

the salt in such an awful place for the mastodon to get to.
Didn't that make them real mad? you are asking. Of course!

But the monument's not to their pain or their anger. It says
they had big bones, like *New Yorker* advertisement models

or tackles, or soldiers. Who were the most famous mastodons?
When a mastodon cleared from the pit stop with hips,

he bellowed and blustered on back at the gods, denied pain and death
while he never looked back. America's sexiest man, a tough mastodon.

Mastodon movements and virtues, religions were bigbig,
with tusks in their prayers and with hair on the schnoz.

They differed in part from the modern elephant by having more teeth,
greater size, and the onus of being eggs stinked. The symbol

they chose for their political party was the mastodon. Now South in Big
Bone Lick State Park the folks travel longlong to commune with bigbig.

We'll hike and we'll gasp and we'll scope the cold fossils
bequeathed by a leghold trap set by the stones and the water

become human heart and brain crusted in bone. Back in the car,
kids. We'll be down there soon. You're gonna like this,

they're dinosaurs, so big they make us look small.

Dueling Field

> *"Looking for a present for your dog or cat? Here*
> *are some gifts that can be found at the Yuppy Puppy:*
> *—Yarmulkes, skullcaps for Jewish dogs $10.95."*
> *   —Moment Magazine, 2/91*

> *"Matthias Poehland has been suspended from the ministry*
> *of the Evangelical and Lutheran Churches of Thuringia*
> *for baptizing cats."*
> *   —The Progressive, 2/91*

The Jewish dog and the Lutheran cat
Side by side on a stone bench sat;
It was early evening, they'd strayed from their path.
A dog and a cat at a Turkish bath!
   And the Persian rug and the Yemeni coat
   Seemed to know that these critters had missed the boat
And were lost without paddles, unclear where they're at.

  (I missed it, too, but here's my plug:
  This scoop was swept from the Persian rug!)

The Jewish dog wept as if lost in Gahana.
The Lutheran cat prayed "Meow," and "Hosana."
Their prayers in the steam rose up high past the ceiling
Ecumenically cleansing all impious feeling.
   The Yemeni coat then proclaimed at the sight
   Of the Protestant cat with the dog Israelite:
"If one was a Hindu, we'd see Indiana!"

  (But don't take my word on this ludicrous quote.
  I tell what was told by the Yemeni coat!)

No seraph descended to show a clear sign
Where cat and dog sogs in warm steam clouds combine

And as in all lands, once they stepped from their perch
They dropped the sweet pose of the choirboy-in-church.
  A howl and a wail and the awfullest cries
  Rose up where their prayers had just aimed for the skies:
"Whose will be done?" "Be it thine?" "No, mine!"

(Typical. Yeah. Now I ain't being smug.
If you're not buying this, then you go ask the rug.)

When wrath comes to prayer or when prayer comes to wrath
We can look at all holy wars' end aftermath.
Where the dog and the cat tore up stubble and ground
Not a whisker or tooth or a claw could be found.
  They consumed one another in pugilist fury:
  A furry apocalypse, and the lone jury
looked on without tears — for there still stood the bath.

(The Yemeni coat it told me so
And that is how I came to know.)

The Wives of the Saints

They're churchgoing matrons who see to the patrons
Of God's True House both where they live and they pray.
Blessed with the knowing of sites where love's flowing
They quiet the devil and speak their soft say.

"Always attendant but never dependant,"
The Ladies Auxilliary Marching-In League
Embarks as the agents of heavenly patience.
Onward, Christian soldiers with battle fatigue!

Saints keep odd, pure hours and righteousness sours
And sometimes the tongue of a saint hath no mirth:
"You watch what you say, fool!" But a husband more faithful
Is not to be found under heaven, o'er earth.

The Wives of the Saints have been handing out taints
Along with indulgences, succor and healing —
Those taints that we ever consider endeavor.
The weakness of flesh, blood, and bone we call "feeling."

NEEDS

*I stand in the church. The congregation has risen to sing
"We shall overcome some day." They have linked hands.
Have I the right to reach out and take hands, too?
 I am not sure. I stand self-conscious.*

—Barbara Deming
"Notes After Birmingham"

A Woolworth's in Sacramento

*What I don't understand is how come half of the world is crying
while the other half of the world is crying too, man.*
—Janis Joplin

Well groomed, the white suburban kid was skateboarding
through the aisles of plastic jewelry. But by the time
I saw him he was prone, one leg at unmuscular odd angle
and the linoleum spread and spatted bright cherry red,
spilled Slushie.
                    That splash of sugar sent one young uniform
for a mop. The kid looked up to upside down faces, sideways faces,
faces of concern from the world's other half.
These were the ones who shopped at Woolworth's,
not the ones who rolled the aisles.
                    That splash of sugar. That wrong
splash on the surface, like the splash from the train car
spilled upriver. Metham sodium pesticide mirrored the crazy
red sugar and dye around this teenager's head as wonder and tears
welled in his darting eyes.
                    Researchers wrote that if a rat
is put into a cage in which it has previously
received an electrical shock, it will start to cry. Was
the pain familiar as the odd angled clerks
                    smoothed their skirts
as they bent in concern? "You going to be okay," intoned one.
Was that a statement or question? Soon paramedics
would busy themselves.
                    The boy would stop being being boy, but would
become injured leg. Still, this was not soon. This was tears
and spilled sugar, with half of the world's wealth looking upward
to neon and plastic, immobile on the floor.
The other half of the world's wealth,
                    pensioners and Woolworth clerks,
the man with a cane but no belt, so part of his butt showed,
the woman dressed in her one dress of old satin

to look nice for Wednesday, for shopping day:
                                     So they ministered.
So deeply they cared if the poor kid was hurting.
So fluid the music, so easily they cried.

24 March 90: White House Snapshots

The smiles cast about settle deep but not wide
and the fog of wet snows makes earth soup on the march.

In ten thousand walking souls, each holds the chaos
of the world in a unit, a sinew, a system.

Away, a train hurtles between towns, rattles windows.
Their crystalllized molecules hum in their work.

And South at San Salvador's National Cathedral
ten thousand more march a foot eulogy for Monsignor

Romero. They march in the face of the rifles
and state of siege. They chant that the army

may cut down the flowers, but won't stop the Spring.
Ten and ten thousand and more tens and tens

and the tension of ten years at war mark the trail.
We pass resolute from the big house, some jailed

and all shivering. Security guards stuff their notes
in their pockets. A moon rises full in a Vietnam night.

Old World Spider

The tarantula, a European spider,
has a delicate sense of touch. Its attack
is swift, so swift the camera can't catch it.
It can react independently of appetite.

To reproduce, the digger wasp Pepsis
will sting the tarantula, and the paralyzed spider
is buried, become a womb for the wasp's larva.
Life to life and injured to spawning, the still-breathing spider

nourishes the new life from the ground.
The tarantula migrated South
and then West, to the country
where you can take a bullet from a Peacekeeper.

The prolific, hairy critter
found homes in land of contradictions,
old chaos and new turf. Viewed in fear and wonder,
it found open space, warm climate.

Brandfort is a small town, but once shaped
the national identity of Dr. Henry Verwoerd,
architect of apartheid law. Here the clinic
is locked, for the nurse has no supplies

or medicine. A banned person might be placed
in the house the builders use to store the rubbish
and held under house arrest, without water or stove.
Outside the shacks is cooler than in through October,

and Nomawethu holds her daughter close, drawing a shawl
to break the dusty wind. For a week
she has fed the child on braised flour,
since there is no money for cereal or fruit.

The help comes sporadically, a food shipment
to the Methodist creche, or a shuttle to the hospital
in Bloemfontein. This was the morning
of pension day. The donkey carts

converged on town from four a.m.
Nomawethu leaves her daughter with her brother for a while;
it is her day to work the garden, a self-help project begun
ever since the drought. "so far,

there is no law against dreaming."
The police station fills on pension day,
recipients who have "created a disturbance in white Brandfort."
They have swelled with the sting,

or have swallowed the ferment of survival.
The spider migrated until the sun
never set on the arachnid empire. Societies know
natural enemies and natural alliances

and these too transform, evolve into opposites.
Having been paralyzed, tarantulas
have been restored to partial mobility
under laboratory conditions, by experts in Western science,

and each time this experiment succeeds,
one larva is lost, an egg in hostile space, unnourished.

Driving Out of Seneca County

Driving out of Darlington County
My eyes seen the glory of the coming of the Lord
Driving out of Darlington County
Seen Wayne handcuffed to the bumper of a state trooper's Ford
—Bruce Springsteen

One day we climbed naked on rocks in high desert.
We tasted the fire once we tasted the acid.
I watched geologic formations slide open.
My skin burned the crimson of pirates and warfare.

Today while I drove over Seneca County
Mandela walked proud on the grounds of the free road
from Victor Verster prison farm back toward Capetown.
My thoughts all burned bright, adolescent mad memory.

My buddies and I, we all saw the goals clearly:
Play loud rock'n'roll and throw out the government.
Today at the Mandela house in Soweto
the green, black, and yellow paint winks at the sun.

We screamed our annoyances, chants and sharp slogans
at business suits, cops, and political rivals.
The process moved forward. One war started ending.
I didn't know then how huge others would blossom,

more hidden and spanked with tough codes for survival.
South of our borders, trees from Indochina
dropped seedlings, and the hateful pears of death.
Vertical bars scar the Southern horizon.

From Seneca County they look like scared soldiers.
Yellow was gold in war contractors' pockets.

Green was the slash of the tropics in torment.
Black was mine dust and the birds on a carcass.

It's Sunday and Seneca County has white sales
and green lawns and kids whizz by laughing
on bright yellow bicycles. A long time ago
Westmoreland sent napalm up and down up and down

to jungles and cities. Mandela was charged
with inciting to strike and was sent to live
out his natural life in the prison on Robben Island.
I was sixteen years old at an antidraft meeting

and the counselor said, "Here's the kind of dumb question
the board throws at you: would you have taken up arms
against Hitler?" So I scrambled a while and the counselor
muttered, "You know, it's like asking if you'd fight

in the War of the Roses." I'm fast pushing forty
and I'm ready to face my old draft board.
The War of the Roses is passing, and royal succession
breathes national gasps. So where's Sixty Seven?

I itch now all over to face the hard stares
of those old guys, declaring my battle's on them.
What did they want with my brains and poor eyesight?
They were mine to abuse and to play with, like now.

I drove where the branches bent low. Must have snowed.
And we keep on walking and we keep on talking,
walking down that freedom road.

The New Brood, Midseason

Where I'm staying, the owls have moved in. The redwing
blackbirds flocked, keeping owls at far distance
the previous months. One night, a trip to a city bookstore
to hear a photographer talk on his new book, documenting
the people's venture in ten years of Sandinista rule.

The row behind me has a new Nicaraguan emigre,
and a young Californian who does a quiet, simultaneous translation
for him. It's quiet before the talk. The Nicaraguan
picks up a book of Diego Rivera's mural work.

> "It's nice, this work. It's very good."
> "Oh, Rivera's great."
> "Did he work a lot?"
> "His stuff's all over. He's a local legend here in San Francisco."
> "He's famous, this artist?"
> "Very famous."

A pause. Book pages shine up in rainbows and gloss,
the wings of the quetzal. The flowers. The lives
where we hope and take air, drowning in history's wind.
The California kid is talking again.

> "You know who this artist is, don't you?"
> "No."
> "This is Frida Kahlo's husband."
> "Oh, I know this artist."

This past week the blackbirds have moved down the hill
to the lagoon, where they'll raise the summer's second brood.
They'll collect and soar with common minds.
Their shadows will skim fast on water through the reeds.
This new part of their lives will be contemporary with egrets
and mallards who preen on old swamp posts.

Coyote and the Flower Farm

I know that you're dissatisfied
With your position and your place.
Can't you understand, it's not my problem?
—"Positively 4th Street"

I.

The bare facts hit at the bare nerves like a mattock:
Edwin Ives, Ventura County farmer, with seven others
lured Mexicans across the border, promising good wages:
pay so high the smuggling fee ($435) would fly
in instants. Nogales to Somi's ranch country brought beatings
and marginal wages, sixteen hour days. A seven
foot fence barricaded the compound where workers
bought food from the company store. They were told
that they might leave when their mushrooming debts
were paid off. One worker, crippled by blows
to the head and the back was sent home.
A C-note was slipped to his hand at the border
to cover all treatment. The year was 1990.
Here's how they farmed flowers *en California sur.*

In April, complaints charged Lnu and Singh, foremen,
with violence. Feds came to investigate. More charges developed:
violations of labor and civil rights laws, as well
as a federal anti-slavery statute. Imagine the trek
a man makes to the land of opportunity. *California!*
Mexico viejo! The Spanish Trail North! What does
he think when the land is fists and wires?

II.

Coyote gave silver to seven of his mudheads dressed in Confederate grey. He was mad at the Pueblo, who could dance in four places at once. He thought he would trick the Pueblo into thinking they lived in the valley of the Hawk Moon and served for an Antelope Priest. Coyote wore an antelope head, but removed the pronghorns so the Pueblo would say "Look. He is not here for fighting. He is here to run and make magic.

The silver was offered Coyote for flowers by the poeple of the North, who do not comb their hair. This was a day when beautiful clouds dotted the sky on the One-Way Trail. He said look, we can get all the metals we want, even the yellow metal that makes people crazy. The mudheads jumped up and down on the soil. "There is no end to the metals we will have!" The mudheads jumped so high that their heads bumped the clouds and thunder rolled and they came down so hard that the earth wrinkled up into valleys without rivers.

The mudheads were not slowed by their uniforms and weapons. The hope of endless metals made their feet fly like birds. In two days they were near to the city where the Pueblo lived. They knew they had to convince the Pueblo that they knew the flower fields in the Valley of the Hawk Moon. What would Coyote do? they asked. He would do a big trick. He would talk like a powerful hawk.

One of the mudheads, the one they called Naju, threw fire on the ground in the Pueblo city. A big cloud came up and in it stood Naju in his neat grey uniform with silver buttons and the beak of a hawk. He carried a large rabbit in his beak and shook it with a fury. He cried a bird cry shrill as a flute. He ran down the street and a trail of red berries followed him. What are you? the Pueblo asked. "I'm the one who comes with the hawk magic. Look!" he said and tore off his uniform. He had grown pubic feathers.

One hundred Pueblo men followed Naju to the edge of the city. There the mudheads explained their trade. "You will come to the Valley of the Hawk Moon, which is in the North Country. The lost white brother Panaha will be coming there when he comes. The land is made ready by the waters we have taken from the mountains. We will feed and lodge you there, and there will be cornmeal for the horses to walk on. The Hawk God wants us to know the beauty of the flowers and and the strength of the traveller, so we will travel to his valley and plant the flowers in rows as far as the eye can see. Panaha will like this, too."

In three days they arrived at the camp Coyote had made. My mudheads did well, thought Coyote, and gave them each corn dolls and arrows soaked with a medicine that smelled bad. What Coyote did not know is that the mudheads were thinking only of the metal they would have, and that the medicine would make them fierce. What Coyote was thinking about was tricking the Pueblo who had come from a far city. Coyote wanted to trade the flowers with the people of the North for himself, see, and he did not want to give anything to the Pueblo. That is why he built a fence around his camp, made of lightning and thistles. It was a powerful magic, that fence.

Well, the travellers got one look at Coyote wearing the antelope head with the horns cut off and they started to laugh and dance all over the place. "Look at old Coyote!" they shouted. "A bag of bones all dressed to run!" Then Coyote thought he would pretend to be Panaha. Old Coyote always thought his enemies and the people he played his tricks on were stupid! He put on checkered pants which covered his tail, so no one would see his furry rump. He put on big shoes with cleats and a shirt made all from chemicals. The shirt was decorated with an arrow, and to look like he had company, it had words: I'M WITH STUPID. He painted his face with white chalk and wore a checkered cap with a milkweed pod on top. He carried a bag of clubs, all skinny and long with with mallets on the end.

Then he walked in front of the Pueblo and made a speech. "There are waters and there is black earth here, this makes me happy. It is good that you have come to this place. But I am not ready to live here with you. This place is destined to be a garden full of flowers. Make it ready for me!" To show how serious he was, he made a mean face and spit out his cracked yellow teeth and rolled over and danced like a crazy dog. This time the disguise worked, and the Pueblo picked up tools and planted flowers.

By now the mudheads were very angry from their medicine and playful with their arrows. While Coyote made his speech they were

shooting corn dolls off rocks and hitting each other. They got
tired of this game and started hitting on and shooting the Pueblo
planting in the fields. Some of the planters told Coyote what was
happening, and he didn't care. So he tried another trick. "I will
stop them!" he promised. The way he stopped them was to give them
some of the yellow metal and cook some rabbits. This made them
quiet for a while, but did not stop the medicine's work. Pretty
soon they were back to attack the planters.

How hard it was for the Pueblo who had travelled so far! They
could not leave the camp because of the fence. Their lodging and
cornmeal were bad. They could not eat the flowers that they
planted, and the rest of their food they had to buy from the
mudheads. What Coyote did not know is that his camp was the talk
of all the animals and people in the other valleys. Even the
hunting people heard about it. They drove cars that could cross
the lightning fence and came hunting for Coyote. They wore silver
badges and carried long revolvers. They saw the mudheads. Look!
said the hunters, they are still wearing the Confederate grey
uniforms we heard about! The hunters put all the mudheads in a
cage and they put the cage in a stone house.

Then they asked the planters if they knew where old Coyote was.
They described skinny and his antelope head. But this is not the
true place of the antelope, they said. Why would you look for
antelope here, asked the hunters. Because the mudhead with the
hawk magic said that this was the place of the Antelope Priest,
and we have seen Panaha here! Even though the hunters knew all
the mudheads were locked up, the mention of Panaha the white
brother gave them a start. They knew this was Coyote's work.

Coyote knew that he'd best disappear, so he started climbing
into the earth on a spider web. But the hunters saw him and
pulled him back up again. They put him in the cage with a bunch
of angry mudheads and drove their big cars over and over the
thistle fence. They even took away the chemical shirt and the clubs.

Now we know Coyote can always get out of a stone house. I think
this time he will say, "I am not Coyote. I am his twin. He asked
me to watch the camp while he traded horses with the Water Clan."
And he will sneak out. He knows a lot of tricks.

Count to Three, Count to Twelve

> *And ten brothers of Joseph went down to buy grain in Egypt.*
> *But Benjamin, Joseph's brother, Jacob sent not with his*
> *brothers; for he said: Lest mischief befall him.*
> **—Genesis XLII: 3-4**

Who knows ten? I know ten.

Ten of twelve brothers were sent to do commerce.
Of two favored brothers, one stayed in the home
of protective belief. With one other enslaved

in a faraway land, Benjamin was select from his siblings'
adventure. What was favor? Reuven asked Dan,
was it breeding or wisdom or youth or ideals?

Sand and stone markers were all of the Sinai.
The way was barren. The harvest was far.
Favor was grain in drought. Favor was land.

Who knows three? I know three.

For there to be a Third World, there must be
a First World. Three are the heroes of the modern
revolution in Nicaragua: Fonseca, Lopez, and Borge.

Three are the Wise Men and Three are the Stooges.
Three are the colors of Old Glory. What was privilege,
Borge asked Fonseca. Was it bleeding or wealth

or a big car or food? *La mariposa,* the butterfly
(for the Maya, a symbol of life) caught a May breeze
from under the leaf where it hid from the rains.

Who knows one?

One is the thin wheel of Ben Linder's unicycle.
One is the iron and gesturing clown in a park in Managua
and one is the mind of the people who tell you

that they too knew a kind *norteamericano* Ben Linder
who talked with them and asked advice and was their friend.
One is the one one who knew everyone and "How could he do that?"

one wonders. One was a generator and one was a light bulb
and one was a filament in country that hadn't seen current before.
One was the wise son, one favor, one privilege.

One kid. Only one kid.

William Walker XVIII

1. San Salvador

Looking no healthier than a swipe for the trotters
and pacers for the track by Del Ray
a brindle dog, "too dead to skin,"
rolls and runs near Walker's feet.
A teenaged girl kicks dust
with her sandals past the *zapateria*
and he breathes sound in warm March winds.

Two months before the rains begin
Walker muses on the curve and fold
of fabric on this *chica's* frame. Another machine
in a machine system. (What do you call
the one who sees wealth where shanties
sweat and insects fly? — A diplomat.)
An echo strains from *la playa*, where

a barracuda's strayed unusually close
to shore. This is the land of exotic animals
bright birds and turquoise lizards
and here a man can work at the factory
and make ninety dollars a month!
William Walker turns and pockets a dream,
a bone, a finger, a life and a stone.

2. The Gates of History

The sign below the gate proclaims
"Ancestors alive in oneself."
Somewhere Walker went out to destroy,

not create the new reality.
Bolivar's coalition dissembled the slave state
that Walker and gunmen set sail to rebuild.
Walker who once was repelled at Honduras

is walking the spine of the books of the new
begging entrance; he eats of the medicine baked
for illusions; he sniffs a white powder
for battles imagined; he tears at the fabric
of frozen reminders and documents printed,
as though history's book would fly open when nagged
long enough. Greed's subterranean streams

bathe his eyelids. Garnets and trinkets of bright
yellow paint start swimming in visions
of what might be treasure. And Walker's ecstatic!
Now he knows that the answer to no way out
will be no way in! He can fold up the uniform
left by his fathers and slip into colors and time
without sound. These gates have been waiting

to close shut without him. The world wet and tropical dims,
and a flight into Texas will leave in an hour.
Wave wave *adios* wave goodbye.

Overdue Letter

The big buildings had now give the place to a more modest ones,
which become more and more rare, until only a little, humble,
odd, funny houses rise here and there from the accidented soil.
O, funny, humble, old little houses that I love; little house always
big enough for the greatest loves, and most saint affections.
Here I see two girls of the people going to work. They look like
to be sisters. Their shoulders are more large than those of the
girls I meet a little before, but little curved. On their pale
faces are lines of sorrow and distress. There is sobberness and
suffering in their big, deep, full eyes. Poor plebian girls, where
are the roses of your springtime?
                          —Bartolomeo Vanzetti
                          (letter to Elizabeth Evans, 1921)

I.

A noche en Managua
by a batteried florescent gasp
and a dictionary, I cut sloppy
flashes of recognition into the Mendozas' copy
of the prison poems of Morales Aviles,
martyr of the revolution.

  Para tí, Doris Maria. Tienes urgencia de
  mi cuerpo, angustia de mi besas.

Está es la estacion de las lluvias
and the iguanas tear lightning tracks
on the rain-buckled boards of Altagracia's
houses. Electric reptile nerves
snap heat and clouds roll through
like cattle.
          The city teems

with the newly arrived — in the country
it can be dangerous. This is not the idyll
of the Italian bee farm you are remembering,
Bartolomeo.
      Children peek-a-boo
around cardboard on concrete floors —
mothers chase the mud away —
the most saint affections.

Foster and his father, exhausted with patrol time,
sit with a pad to juggle time
arranging for both to be home for two weeks.
Free will isn't any cheaper in Rio Coco
than Braintree.

II.

   sobberness and suffering
   in their big, deep, full eyes

Can you picture the eyes still, Bartolomeo,
through the blind spot woven into the big, deep retina
by the cell's single bulb?
On the revolutionary anniversary — the 4th of July —
I watched the National Chorus
sing from Coca-Cola risers
the lyrics from Ruben Dario and Swing Low
Sweet Chariot
      A chestnut *muchacho*
moved forward to play at riser's edge.
Sitting straight at first with legs spread,
he leaned slowly forward
and eventually curled, to sleep
close to where his father was singing.

He had full eyes.

No matter what the photographer says,
my dad told me before the class picture,
don't smile for the camera.
You only look handsome when you're serious.

III.

Late into the night Francisco
continues to document the route
        past Leon into the mountains
though fictions and truths
        are malleable angels in his mouth.
Francisco's eyes run deep and brown
like the rivers to the North.

"And there were these gringos
who fought side by side with Borge,
Howard and Roger. Howard was from Kansas City.
Roger was from New Mexico.
They used to make films about the Holocaust
        and in Matagalpa they taught many Spanish
        people to write. Now they are in El Salvador."

I have been trying to keep up
y tengo cansado. Cooksmoke
carries nitrogen from the living wood
along walls to the heavens.
        Downstairs, Mathilde and Gloria
        — their shoulders little curved —
        arrange plates, food, clothing
        in the order they go to the basin.

Francisco draws deep breath. "You know, in those days
the headless bodies in the street
were commonplace. In 1978 alone

more than 500 students and professors were killed
and thousands jailed. The Guard was crazy then
and no one knew what home they'd invade next.
Some were conscious of the need
for political support and look!" — he points.
"The cockroach!"
                        I jerk forward, awake
as a brute crashes down the wall.

Sonreimos. Acrid air sweetens
with roses of springtime.

IV.

In the field that stays dusty
at the bend of the road to Juigalpa
eight-year-old Marlon trips fast
            over rocks and hoists
            his tired smudge of kite
with the wind.
            The kite's made of brand-new
            newspaper clumps.
Farmers ride by on saddled oxen.
The names of the new casualties
La Guardia has taken
            flit above their heads, fragile
            as fireflies
            — truths always are —
cast to earth through Marlon
who pitches the skies.

The grey print on grey sky in summer gusts
would enchant you, Bartolomeo.
Kilometers where the big buildings

have give place to a more modest ones
are a path to the mountains for Marlon.
A cattle man from Mexico
fumes past, delivering a new Isuzu truck
with the price marked down
because of the bullet holes.
The scent of the city
comes close for a moment,
   then steams into the soil like urine,
   like the ghosts of the newly dead.

V.

Augustin's got a razor
and Robertin's got fast hands.
On the way to Rigoberto Lopez stadium
before the baseball game with Panama
they cleared paper, twenty-six dollars,
four thousand three hundred and sixty cordobas,
pictures of two saints
and a torn, empty wallet.

Claudia comes to discuss how frightened she becomes
about what the children learn
when Francisco hits Gloria.
Why doesn't God intervene, she wants
to know. I come from a capitalist country
where frustrated people drink
and will hit each other also, I say.
Well, it's different for you.
You come from a smart country
ruled by the underdeveloped religion
of Protestantism. Claudia only cries
for less than a minute, but it brings
Cristal, running. She always

cries with her mother, her mother
who wrestles tentacles of evil.

Evil falls on our kind like snow
on the branch. The branch becomes weighty
and tired, and bends.
The snow falls of its own weight.
The branch springs back strong.

They have snow in the mountains sometimes,
Claudia tells me. I hear too
that there is much snow where you come from.

VI.

At the month when the troops secured Leon
Rebecca showed me the spot
in Mt. Airy Forest
where the Wyoming High School kids
went out to get high. Under flickering sun
we played with a dagonfly.
She had descended from James Joyce —
someplace in his family, anyway —
and was looking forward to reading him.
She had ulcers set against argument
and stress, and bad doctors.

Already the corner
Where Pedro Joacin Chamorro had taken his bullet
was a shrine. Old bouquets
would kiss the hot winds. When Pastora
abandoned the greed mill
and dollar-squabbling of the mercenary armies
we were racing steep roads —

Wasn't that a time. Then.
Not long ago the late frost choked
life from April blossoms. In Ohio
I brought roses to Rebecca's spot of soil.
Her parents were so proud
of their daughter's education
they had the shield of a registered nurse
carved into the marker.

It's no longer news that the greedy
have no martyrs.
Saints speak a foreign language
in the boardrooms. They're
lucid in the fields.
In old Managua
the air is always perfumed
above Chamorro's corner.

And in your story, Bartolomeo?
Here's an update on the one
who passed your sentence in Boston:
Judge Webster Thayer's ashes
sour the clay in blistered earth.

VII.

Sandino springs to wood doors everywhere.
The woodworms know his name.

VIII.

Where leaf and paper touch sunny ground
a semiphore of shadow signals

from a barbed wire clothesline
to spiders and ants. The t-shirts
all the young of the family wear,
   black collar   red sleeve:
   Aqui esta su cachorro.
Inanimate clothes and dust are alive
in this wind.

Mathilde and Abuelita talk about you
with Francisco, who studied the shootings
at South Braintree for his Labor Day program.
Then he saw a movie made in Italy
on the television about your defense.
A roach flew up at the screen while Joan Baez
sang across the soundtrack's static.

Abuelita hugs Mathilde from behind,
close and long, and sighs.
They look like to be sisters.

I feel suddenly aware that the smell
of beauty crushing against ugly,
the smell of woodsmoke and gasoline,
sprouting plants and somebody's vomit
are common city air in North and South alike.
Boston's bay winds play
new wrinkles into t-shirts there.

I'm sorry it took me seventy years
to write you, Bartolomeo.
The time was probably right before.
And here we are again.

                VII '88
                Nicaragua Libre

Needles and Needs

Somewhere this side of the Plaza España
I ducked from the rain to a steamy cafe
where I tried to imagine if Nicaraguans
were ever exposed to the Marx Brothers.
I had brought the red shirt which bore the design
that our leftists display with the lineup, all four:
Groucho, Harpo, Chico and Carlos.
"Sure, I'm a Marxist!" cries the inscription.
I thought it would make a nice gift
for Antonio, who's been a swell host.
That is, if the graphic would make any sense.
I asked of the waiter, "Sir, with your permission,
I've a question of curiosity, of panamerican culture.
Do you recognize these stars of the *ciné, Los Hermanos Marx.*
They were very funny. They made a lot of films
in the '30s. Very popular guys, and famous in my country.
"No, I don't know them," he told me. "But wait.
I'll ask my friend."

I downed some beers with Martin and Jeff, guys
studying Spanish and spending some days as U.S. marines
charging hills by Masaya in a film biography of Sandino.
The storm was deep rivers, then tropical bellows,
then puffs of lost rainbows. I breathed the rich air
washed of diesel and smoke. In the skeleton district
Sandino's men weep as they bundle their uniforms
for Mexican haven, the uniforms they wear to church.
You can hear it in mariachi songs and in motors.
Their blood is the red fruit, *pitaya,* on marble.
That was clear as the glasses clinked hollower, then
Martin had some harsh words for Littin, the celebrated
director who had Marines spread out and fire in a pattern
that with live ammunition, would have had the soldiers
shooting each other in the back. Well, the air looked clear
and we settled our bill, and got up to leave. Our waiter
came running. "*Esperá.* Wait. We have a telephone here.

Maria Elena, she talks to the operator. We're looking to see
if we can find your friends, these Marx Brothers."

Then here is another degree of some value:
There's a factory run by a collective near Jiloya.
On night shift the work slows, and a sloth climbs the hill
above the lagoon and leaves glisten under banana moon.
Estel chairs the union, leans over a table, and shows me
a needle. The air's thick with fibers that sweat, bunch,
and cling. Doctor Che gazes up from an old and torn poster,
looking frail in a white cotton beard. The plant
makes gauze bandage and diapers and swabs and toilet paper.
"You see this needle? It's a tooth from that comb we use
to clean out the cotton." I look at the combing machine;
it's a monster. All afternoon we'd toured through the classrooms
and day care center the workers had founded.
We saw the machines which were used when acquired
from Italy decades ago: now the gears are hard wood
shaped in the shop from hard and deep grained Atlantic Coast trees.
The big comb is silent. The stock of swabs has been dwindling fast.
Dust swells the metal and birds call in iron.

"A mother was swabbing her baby's face in Guatemala.
Her child was cut by this needle. The needle came loose
from that comb. We're supposed to replace the comb
about every year and a half, but we have to tool the part.
That's expensive. Now a baby's been hurt.
We can't run our machine. Between all our shifts
more than two hundred workers have nothing to do. Not until
we find money to make the new part." In the city, many homes
sell cokes or take laundry. Up North, the warehouses
are emptying toxins to rail cars bound South. And an Indian
baby's laid off all these workers. I don't know quite what
to say to Estel. But she is off onto another subject,
relating a strike at a private plantation. It's harder to talk
when denial's outweighed by needles and needs. They say
miracles happen like June rains and freedom. Maria Elena
may reach Harpo yet, and when he's on the line muteness
knows the clear pattern of cotton in wind.

The Music of Asian Carolina

A silver tear appearing now — I'm crying, ain't I?
Gone to Carolina in my mind.
—James Taylor

A Tuvan throat singer in central Asia
generates three tones in his love call,
alternating the strains with a mouth harp.

Some of the song is made of words,
and some imitates the crickets and birds.
His accompanist plays a three string guitar.

The Tuvan throat song confronts modernity
In the past twenty years, women have trained
in the art. Koreans still thrill

to the P'ansori, their epic vocal form.
Balinese street musicians thrum counts of eight
in small percussion ensembles, the gamelan.

Last night I was calling your name, sending a message
through mazes of water and lightning. An age
passes, but come the late morning

children play water polo in the low
lying lawns on Old Fostoria Road.
Mr. Woon checks the water level of his basement,

cursing that he never connected his sump.
And I hear his song harmonize, resonate
in the million human chants

blocked by chances and water, torrents and tears.
Any distinctness sounds miracles in the lonely
shards of creation. And if an only

note gets heard of every many generated,
then the throat song works. A good song
might be an opera or a mop on the spotted tile —

the trick's in the unexpected echo, the sudden recognition,
the recovery,
the recovery.

That's why the Tuvans find their discipline
in constraint. The art is the pressure
that seeks for creation, a bigger job than healing.

Struggling and soggy, the sounds ricochet
by towns from Moscow to Cary out,
across buckeyes and Carolina pines and the watercolor

set in the kitchen. Soundings
formed in the throat, moving South and rising,
recreationg themselves in faith, stubborn faith.

Sometimes the song is an engine or a cricket
and sometimes the strain of an underused spigot.
The force that makes the music is almost arbitrary.

The message is in calling the force to order,
and a message becomes one on being heard.
Rains are due again in the North country,

and Canadian Geese. Cries and whispers. Guitars.

(for Christina)

Kanawha Grey Morning

> *Now nothing remains for building or burning.*
> *The losing of lovers was all I was learning.*
> *A time for escape and a time for returning had come to me.*
> —Phil Ochs, "When in Rome"

I.

Between sharp, unforgiving coal hills Kanawha Valley
(*What do stars answer? Wink. Wink.*)
There seemed a moment to further split greys:

Split hairs, the grey hairs!
Split the grey machine valley wide!
Split grey river from shoreline!

Time was tasting of metal. Everywhere
The troops were taking broadaxes to circumstance.
From Sumter and Bragg, the children

Mustered for far desert country. A young woman's
Exhusband and fiance roomed together at base,
And when the marching orders came for the husband to be

Letters were returning. What do soldiers say?
"I don't know what I'm doing here." Of course not.
Uriah dispatched to the front out of sexual jealosy,

So God retaliated, took David and Bathsheba's firstborn.
And now children pursue more vituperous whims,
Their shields a vaccine in the bloodstream

Their weapons all raised in defense of grey sludge.
Not even their own grey sludge. Kanawha grey morning's
Been breathing cold soot. The power plant

Onriver chugs drumsound looking for the passion
Of the skins which live all around.
Kanawha grey morning wants lovers together.

Kanawha grey morning brews cofee from banksoil.
Kanawha grey morning is hungry for greyslag.
Kanawha grey morning sighs old in frost jacket.

Kanawha grey morning sends ice with its water.
Kanawha grey morning seeks fire in the winter.
Kanawha grey morning loves the tickle of deer, tripping

Through its roads and toothpicks, the splinter of trees
Which were reaching for the moon, or have fallen from it.
A landscape of hopes built from splinters, splinters

From hopes. The woman's exhusband and fiance
Are named John. They are the same man and he has two bodies.
(This is no riddle. A barracks or war tent can never distinguish

From conscript to conscript. That's why there are uniforms.)
Kanawha grey morning is watching the travelers
And starting to dress in the paints of its day.

It once saw the brute shoat of warfare at play.
There was blood. Some animals don't comprehend children.
They're just nasty.

II.

Joe Dallet, first husband to Kitty Oppenheimer, was martyred
on the altar of Free Spain. A disciplined man who took soldiering
seriously, he became an expert on the maintenance of machine guns.
Relaxed in the evenings, the day's drills behind him, he spoke
of his guns with respect and with love. And fifty years after
his death in defense of the sainted and dying republic, a new
democratic Spain voted United States missiles from their ground.

Kitty danced a slow waltz of devotion and meaning between Joe's guns
and Robert's bombs. Tides covered the obstinate bones of fishermen
and farmers. Warfare then could mean the comfort of mourning,
almost a romantic notion in these echoes and sirens of anger. Today
Robert's bombs sail the oceans and circle the planet. They've been shrunk
small as handlaunched mortars. They've been swelled large as buildings.
And we waltz the country waltzes. The dance of the old country.
Any old country.

III.

Past Grimm's Landing and Hometown the poplars —*los alamos* —
mix with scrub pine and beech trees. The poplar grows quickly,
and mixes with hardwood growth. Today is a season of many raccoons
and few leaves. The drive through Kanawha grey morning filled
with folk music from a little tape machine and the singers
were all of them for peace. "If God's on our side, he'll stop
the next war," they would sing. Last night's last stars
were winking out. Were it given to me to write the script,
then what would it say? Wink. Wink. It would try to describe
the shadings and lustres of grey, stretching back past the bottles
of iron filings in the chemistry set, back to dinosaur skins.
It would try to record the slow change of the day which *isssssss*
after *allllll* a day like all others. A day born to tinker small
chemical changes, little surges of plasms and synthesis of energies.
Slight black clouds mark their landfall with lightning up high
on the hillside. This history too is one version of fiction,
but this story's written as light breaks through cloudcover.
Quiltcolors. Big shapes and patches, loose fabrics unbound
and ready to rearrange into constructions that keep us warm.
In this script we're all safe through Kanawha grey morning.
No weapons are written into the story. The lovers get to be
together. With each other. With their children. And day
comes to brightness, safe times for the traveler. Safe even
for the small animals who dart across the roadway.
                                        Playing
inscrutable games.

The Sendings Away

*We stand with you, sir. We love your
adherence to democratic principles and
democratic processes.*
　　　—Vice President Bush, toasting
　　Phillipine President Marcos' electoral victory, 1981

I.

How light and breezy, how dizzy and foolish the flies
in a killing jar, those democrats. As free
from atmosphere as from history —
see them flutter and stumble, doomed shooting stars
in a gallery of high sounding words
all printed on night.

How sputtery and sudden, the flash and the noise —
how the sting disappears as they crumple into the torn
filaments of their wings. Shall we name them?
Those who were not names before? Shall we count
those who counted before as brothers, community guilt
purged in a moment of atonement?
Shall we cast these wings
into the water on days of fasting?

How righteous we were, the procession from synagogue to pond
where we'd cast our crumbs like pollen from anther and sing
and sing and the crumbs were sin and the ducks loved to snap the sin
in their bills before it could leave the surface skein of weed
and dirt. The darkness was coming and the whole scene
was solemn and grown-up and we remembered Babylon.

II.

The men of the temple were sort of an army,
their chant was a sort of release to the sun.
The mud at the pond's edge was sort of an altar,

75

The sort of our sins was the order we'd brought.
"Let them be named, cast forth and atoned for."

I imagined corruption made bread by the magic
of words before God. My nose felt cold
and a wind from the inside of the moon shook the water.
I think this year — again — of what we cast forth:
Crusts for duck, flies for fish, breath for the trees
and the grass. What needs atonement?
  It is less than a week now since the Book of Life
was sealed. Who is to prosper
and who is to die by wild animals. Let them be named.

  Fred Malek, who purged the Jews from the Labor Department.
  Bhodan Fedorak, who spits vinegar when the Justice Department
    threatens to deport fugitives from the Eastern Bloc,
  Ignatius Bilinski, Ukranian Congress of America,
    and honorary co-chair, Coalition of American Nationalities.
  Jerome Brentar, co-chair of Coalition of American Nationalities,
    who denies the Holocaust.
  Radi Slavov, veteran of the Nazi Bulgarian Legion and co-chair,
    Bulgarians for Bush.
  Father Florian Galdau of the Romanian Iron Guard.
  Laszlo Pastor, Hungarian Arrow Cross, junior envoy to Berlin 1937-44.
  Phillip Guarino, of the fascist Italian P-2 Lodge.

The water is still. We have carried them all.

III.

A song of ascension.

Though the ones who hate without reason
are more numerous than the hairs on my head,
I shall not fear the terrors that fly by night
or the arrow that flies by day.

This remains a land of wilderness. Gray mastiffs patrol
hotels where the dinner patrons hand thousands of dollars
to buzzards and jackals. Their soldiers hold back the faithful
like stubble driven by the wind. They advance in darkness
like moles.

The moon face of greed and the squealing of pigs mark the road
toward the place of harvest. Be not scared or soiled.

Cobb's Hill Pond was a big place to a ten year old, big enough
to swallow every year's slander and theft. The men will come
to that place again, shiver and cant and cry. When they return
to the temple, they will talk business. The ducks will go South.
The pond surface will freeze, and below it fish eggs will mature
and await a new season.

En afición, está despedida

Yo muchas veces me he perdido
para buscar la quemadura que mantiene despiertas las cosas
—Federico Garcia Lorca

Claudia now has her papers to enter Canada,
and will apply for asylum while staying with kin
in Ottawa. Tonight she wears taffeta, almost the orange
that schoolchildren wear, almost the pumpkin
she wore when detained for six months
in *el corallon*, under guards armed with hollow point bullets
and lofty speeches. Their ears echo threats to the one
decent job the hot Rio Grande has offered their families
for generations of aching *el norte'*s good life.

Claudia remembers everything. She describes brief encounters
in great animation, and smiles an expression that Hollywood
would envy. San Salvador spins into limbos of stubble
and blood as her wellwishers push their addresses
and cards to the table before her. Expectations have grown
in geologic time in her eyes. The birth into "legal"
is the artery of the possible. Maribel prepares for the parting
of journeys they've taken together thus far in new cultures.
Maribel's children may be joined with her soon,
generations transferring the free breaths and roses.

The signboards and railroads.
In the river that flows next to Claudia's party
the tadpoles find evening sun's warmth in gold waters.
In such tiny circles they burn for their life on the earth.

NOTES

"Five and Ten": *Rabochy Put,* the Bolshevik newspaper, renamed *Pravda.* The paper was able to publish continuously until closed briefly by President Yeltsin in October, 1993.

"Animal Heat": *Der Tag* and the *Forward* were the leading newspapers for Yiddish-speaking immigrants. *Havdalah* is the liturgy marking the close of the Sabbath.

"First Dance with the Jaguar": The quotation from Hinojosa says, "The only eternal is the sky and the wind and yesterday's heart." A *"soldado"* is a soldier.

"Skink": Beginning in the early 1870s, Pinkertons and mining officials postulated a secret society of Irish terrorists among Pennsylvania mining organizations, the "Molly Maguires." The conspiracy charge gave the owners generous opportunity to jail organizers on vague charges.

"On the Death of William B. Shockley": Shockley, a Nobel laureate for his work on developing the transistor, became a theorist on genetics. "Dysgenics," the cause he championed, made him a hero to white supremicists.

"Old World Spider": The sources for the poem are Alexander Petrunkevich's article "The Spider and the Wasp" in *Scientific American* and Winnie Mandela's *Part of My Soul Went With Him* (Norton, 1984).

"Count to Three, Count to Twelve": In 1987, engineer Ben Linder became the first U.S. civilian combat casualty of the contra war.

"William Walker XVIII": "Falangist" William Walker led the first U.S. military invasions of Nicaragua in the 1850s. His mission to impose a slave economy in Nicaragua, Walker briefly proclaimed himself President. He was executed in Honduras, 1860. The name William Walker reemerged in the late 1980s as the moniker for George Bush's ambassador to El Salvador.

"Overdue Letter": The quotation from Bartolomeo Vanzetti is from *The Letters of Sacco and Vanzetti* (Viking, 1928). The quotation from Morales Aviles translates, "For you, Doris Maria. You hold the intensity of my body, the anguish of my kisses." Other phrases: *Está es la estacion de las lluvias* (It is the rainy season); *y tengo cansado* (and I'm tired); *Sonreimos* (We smile); *Aquí está su cachorro* (Here's your combat hat).

Two significant historical references in the poem are to August Cesar Sandino, who assembled the peasant army in 1927 to oppose U.S. occupation forces and to Pedro Joaquin Chamorro, *La Prensa* editor whose assassination in 1978 served as a fuse reigniting the Sandinista uprising.

"En afición, está despedida": The Lorca quotation, from *Poet in New York,* translates, "I've often lost myself in order to find the burn that keeps everything awake." *"El corallon,"* the corral, is the refugee center — more a detention center than a port of immigration — run by the Immigration and Naturalization Service at Port Isabel.

(Photo by Lisa Williams)

David Shevin has published widely as a journalist, essayist and poet. His writings have won him a 1994 National Endowment for the Arts Fellowship and several individual artist awards from the Ohio Arts Council. His *Discovery of Fire* (Bottom Dog Press, 1988) was chosen for the Ohioana Poetry Award. Among his other books are *The Stop Book* (1978), *What Happens* (1983), and the much praised satirical volume *GROWL and Other Poems: An Anthology by the Pets of the Great Poets* (Carpenter Press, 1990). He has edited *A Red Shadow of Steel Mills: Photos and Poems* (Bottom Dog Press, 1991).

Always active in issues of social justice, the author was recently honored by the city of Tiffin, Ohio, and by the NAACP. He is an Associate Professor of English at Tiffin University.

"If you want to know the sharpness and the coldness of the knife that went through the heart of American leftists when the Soviet Union collapsed, you have to look no farther than these words. But, at the same time, the anger, hope and love that have animated American progressives shine here with undiminished strength.The particulars of America, a durable, justice-loving America, pour forth their lights in David Shevin's poems. He is an unsparing keeper of the socialist record but also a whimsical human with a humor older than America or himself."

—Andrei Codrescu